# NEW ORLEANS
# THEN & NOW

# NEW ORLEANS THEN & NOW

LESTER SULLIVAN

THUNDER BAY
P·R·E·S·S

San Diego, California

**Thunder Bay Press**
An imprint of the Advantage Publishers Group
5880 Oberlin Drive, San Diego, CA 92121-4794
www.thunderbaybooks.com

Produced by PRC Publishing,
The Chrysalis Building, Bramley Road, London W10 6SP

An imprint of **Chrysalis** Books Group plc

Library of Congress Cataloging-in-Publication Data.

Sullivan, Lester.
   New Orleans then & now / Lester Sullivan.
      p. cm.
   ISBN 1-57145-983-9
   1. New Orleans (La.)--Pictorial works. 2. New Orleans (La.)--History--Pictorial works. I. Title: New Orleans then and now. II. Title.

F379.N543585 2003
976.3'35'00222--dc21                                              200340987

PRINTED IN CHINA

2 3 4 5 6 08 07 06 05 04

To Simon Clay

**ACKNOWLEDGMENTS:**
The author wishes to thank the staffs of two rich repositories for access to the historical images reproduced herein. With a few exceptions, the "Then" views are divided equally between the Library of Congress (LC) and the Historic New Orleans Collection (HNOC). The earliest views come from the HNOC. Founded in 1966 by General and Mrs. L. Kemper Williams, the repository has assembled the largest holding anywhere of imagery on New Orleans. The Collection's J. Dearborn Edwards photographs date from about 1858, making them the earliest known paper prints, excluding portraits, to have survived from the New Orleans area. They represent a unique window into the way of life before the Civil War. Among the HNOC's post-bellum views of the city used in this book are two stereographs, the old-fashioned three-dimensional pictures such as featured in great-grandma's parlor. The remainder of the views from the Collection were taken early in the twentieth century by Charles L. Franck, a leading local commercial photographer. Particular thanks go to HNOC staff member John Magill, who knows more about the history of the physical infrastructure of New Orleans than anyone else. As for LC, it holds over twenty-five thousand views from the Detroit Publishing Company, one of the largest firms publishing photographs in the United States from the late 1890s until the end of World War I. The glass plates range in size from 6 x 8 to 18 x 22 inches and have yielded highly detailed images for the present volume. Thanks to the efforts of LC staff members, the full range of these stock images can be accessed via the American Memory web site at http://memory.loc.gov/ammem/detroit/dethome.html.

# INTRODUCTION

Home of Mardi Gras madness, birthplace of jazz, and host to the internationally popular Jazz & Heritage Festival, one among the handful of top tourist destinations in the nation, New Orleans has been rightly called "the City that Care Forgot." When you think New Orleans, you think partying. When, however, the French founded the place in 1718, they also inadvertently interjected into the party an element of fatalism, fatalism in the face of natural forces.

New Orleans has been called by urban geographer Peirce F. Lewis "the impossible but inevitable city." "Impossible" because no one in his right mind would build a city in the midst of a hurricane-prone and disease-ridden swampland, continually subsiding below sea level. "Inevitable" because the French founders, seeking to establish a trading post to control access to the mighty Mississippi River, could find no alternative. The crescent-shaped sliver of dry land chosen for New Orleans, alongside the deepest spot in the river, was the only natural high ground midway between geographic extremes.

Mobile and Biloxi, the French colonial settlements on the northern shore of the Gulf of Mexico, were located too far to the east to control entry to the mouth of the river. Baton Rouge lay too far upriver. The river itself, unlike many major river systems, does not end in a protected bay, but rather a constantly shifting series of mudflats and sandbars. The channel is very treacherous to navigate and the low-lying land adjacent to it is difficult to build on. To this day, special river pilots must reach Pilottown only by air or water in order to replace the regular pilots of oceangoing vessels, so that ships can negotiate the sixty-mile route winding northward to reach the port.

French colonial New Orleans also had the advantage of a back door via Bayou St. John, through Lake Pontchartrain to the Gulf. It was thus that a Native American trading spot, the portage between lake and river, became an isolated, minor colonial outpost. After a generation or so, the native-born people, the Creoles, arose from a mélange of desperate émigrés. White settlers were acquired from the mother country's own prisons, black ones from the hands of Senegambian slave traders. After their lust for Native American land ended in disastrous war in the 1730s, the French basically turned their focus away from New Orleans.

When, as a result of the Seven Years War, Louisiana in 1763 was transferred to Spanish control, New Orleans became the center of an even more laissez-faire colonial administration. Smuggling in contravention of Spanish colonial law and the size of the racially mixed and free black populations grew exponentially. Two great fires in the 1780s and 1790s almost leveled the town. That's when the original village, the French Quarter, became more Hispanic in appearance. In 1803, Napoleon Bonaparte secretly retook the colony in conjunction with his plan to retake Haiti on the island of Hispaniola. His failure to defeat the rebellious slaves of this former French sugar colony, coupled with his need for ready cash to make war in Europe and his fear of defending Louisiana from encroaching American power, prompted Napoleon to sell the entire Louisiana colony to the United States for four cents an acre.

American rule brought freedom of religion, free trade, and the largest domestic slave-trading market in the country. It also brought opposition to what became the wealthiest free black population in the nation before the Civil War and nagging culture wars between the English-speaking Protestant Americans and the French-speaking Roman Catholic Creoles. The two sides proved amenable to fighting side by side in 1815 in the Battle of New Orleans. However, the ethnic cultural divide became so pronounced that, from 1836 to 1852, New Orleans was sliced into three separate municipalities—two Creole, which eventually grew into backwaters, and one American, which became the boomtown port. The city had entered the great age of steam, when riverboats funneled the massive produce of the vast Mississippi Valley through the Crescent City. The broad expanse of Canal Street became the great dividing line between the ethnically differing neighborhoods, and both the Quarter and the American Sector filled up with imposing Greek Revival edifices encrusted with elaborate cast-iron curlicues.

By the middle to late 1850s, growth in the economy was starting to slow. It is from this era that the earliest photographs in this book date. A new application of steam power in the form of transcontinental railroads revolutionized trade, supplanting the north-south trade axis that advantaged New Orleans with an east-west one that did not. At the same time, New York and other East Coast banks were fast outstripping local banks and growing conflict between pro- and antislavery forces foretold war. The Confederate city fell early to the Union, in 1862, and Reconstruction started earlier, lasted longer, and went further there than anywhere else in the South. The withdrawal of Federal troops in 1876 ultimately ushered in the "separate but unequal" Jim Crow system of legalized racial segregation. The Gilded Age yielded the storied brothels of Storyville, the legalized red-light district and hotbed of ragtime and jazz, not to be shut down until World War I.

Most of the historical views in the book date from a century ago, when the city still extended only twenty or so blocks from the Mississippi River levee. A new kind of high-capacity pump designed by Baldwin Wood made it possible to drain the outlying swamps for land reclamation all the way to the Lake Pontchartrain shore. The Quarter had become a slum, generating the idea of the Vieux Carre Commission and one of America's first historic preservation districts.

World War II brought an end to the Great Depression and the development of a defense industry that produced the landing craft for D-Day. Today, the city is home to the National D-Day Museum. Postwar highway building and suburbanization expanded the boundaries of the metro region. Containerization of cargo transformed the port. Dock workers were displaced, but new employment came elsewhere in the form of service jobs. The "now" pictures reflect that much of the riverfront is now given over to tourism and facilities developed for locals have been turned over for use by visitors.

Both the "then" and the "now" pictures show the lingering evidence of the boomtown days before the Civil War, when New Orleans, not Houston, Dallas, or Atlanta, was the Queen City of the South and was one of the four or five largest cities in the country. The Quarter offers present-day views differing only incidentally from their old-time equivalents, but other parts of town, such as the Central Business District and outlying areas, show much more change. They also show the innate conflicts between progress and preservation in a community notorious for putting the emphasis on heritage, while still trying to confront daunting environmental challenges and keep an old river town economically above water in the twenty-first century.

New Orleans from the harbor, circa 1900. French Canadian Jean Baptiste LeMoyne, Sieur de Bienville, observed the Native Americans' use of a small, crescent-shaped slice of high ground beside a bend in the Mississippi as a land route, or portage, between the river and Lake Pontchartrain. He chose this ten-foot natural levee, which has since been greatly enhanced, for a colonial trading post. In the Crescent City, unlike other river towns, you go up to the river, not down.

A harbor fireboat spouts off, while restoration work proceeds on the southernmost spire of the Saint Louis Cathedral. The relative absence of port facilities and activities as compared with this stretch of the river a century earlier, along with the redevelopment of the Jackson Brewery downriver from the cathedral for retail shopping, reflects an overall shift toward tourism.

A steam-driven ferry at Algiers on the West Bank of the Mississippi. The French founded this area—even before New Orleans—as the location of the great African slave encampment, the Company of the Indies, the firm that ran the colony of Louisiana for the French crown in the early 1700s. This is one of four photos forming a panorama of the city that was made by the Detroit Publishing Company in about 1900.

Today's ferry landing differs somewhat in location because Algiers Point, as a cutting bank of the Mississippi, has lost land to the river. Automobiles and pedestrians are served by a diesel-driven ferry, which is just one of three remaining, along with those at Chalmette and Jackson Avenue, since the construction of the Crescent City Connection—the fourth most heavily traveled toll bridge in the U.S., carrying some 80,000 vehicles daily. Amazingly, there was no bridge in New Orleans until the first of two spans was built in 1958.

Algiers became a municipality in 1842 and was absorbed into the city of New Orleans during Reconstruction in 1870 as the Fifth Municipal District. The old Duvergé House was built by Barthelemy Duvergé in Algiers Point when Louisiana became a state in 1812. A French Creole–style plantation house, it started serving as a courthouse in 1869. It was largely copied in the design for the Louisiana State Building at the World's Columbian Exposition in Chicago in 1893.

The great Algiers fire of 1895 leveled most of the neighborhood, the Duvergé House included. The Hispano Moresque–Revival Algiers Courthouse that replaced it, with its twin crenellated turrets—a familiar landmark from downtown New Orleans, was constructed within the same year. Today it also serves as a museum space and a favorite venue for meetings of local historical societies, including its own Friends of the Courthouse group.

Algiers Bend from the East Bank, a sharp right-angle turn in the Mississippi that is forever cutting away at Algiers Point. The picture, taken circa 1900, shows bulky off-loading equipment on the levee along the Vieux Carré, or Old Square, on the East Bank that today is no longer present. Businesses on the West Bank opposite the city were then more actively engaged in supporting the port through shipbuilding and repair.

The mighty Mississippi is still very much a part of the sights and sounds on both sides of the river, from the whistles of passing paddle wheelers to the awe-inspiring image of oceangoing vessels towering high above the levee. The contemporary view shows change on both banks, with the Aquarium of the Americas and Woldenberg Park drawing tourists in the foreground and a significantly foreshortened point receding in the distance.

010988. PANORAMA OF NEW ORLEANS, LOUISIANA.

The French Quarter, circa 1906, prior to demolition of the old St. Louis Hotel, which functioned during Reconstruction as the state capitol. Probably photographed from the ten-story Old Filter House of the American Sugar Refinery, the hotel may be seen all the way to the left. Damaged in the 1915 hurricane—such storms remained unnamed then—it is now the site of the 1960 Royal Orleans Hotel. In the foreground, warehouses then serving the port dominate the view.

On the left today is the 1909 Beaux-Arts Civil Courts Building. The City Beautiful movement had but a modest impact on the cash-poor New Orleans of the early twentieth century. A major exception was the Courts Building, a product of city planners' neoclassicism inspired by the White City of the 1893 Chicago World's Fair. In the foreground, most of the nineteenth-century warehouses have been obliterated from the area in favor of parking lots and tourist-oriented shopping.

A milk cart in front of the Restaurant de la Louisiane on Iberville. The street is named for Pierre LeMoyne, Sieur de Iberville, the founder of Louisiana who designated New Orleans as its capital in 1723. The cart also delivered Creole cream cheese—a light, fresh, farmhouse-style cheese midway between ricotta and crème fraîche, with an underlying hint of buttermilk. Once de rigueur as part of a Creole breakfast, it is usually served sweetened.

Gone is the old Creole restaurant and instead there is a drive-in entrance for the parking garage that replaced the adjoining Solari's building in the 1960s. The pressure was on to provide greater parking within the tiny grid of the original colonial village, then becoming an ever greater tourist attraction. Today the French Quarter is much less residential and much more commercial than it was a half-century earlier.

In 1864, this quiet corner was transformed into Solari's Market and was for a century the preeminent Creole grocery, widely known for its delicacies. People came from all over New Orleans to eat at the soda fountain and lunch counter, surrounded by cases and shelves brimming with fragrant and colorful fruits and vegetables out of season, rare liquors, and European candies and cookies. The Italianate building's doors closed in 1961.

The parking garage that replaced Solari's is a prime example of what historian Malcolm Heard calls the Vieux Carré Revival, a new architectural style seeking to combine various design elements, sometimes arbitrarily, from earlier French Quarter buildings in a new structure. The idea is that infill should be scenographic and span gaps in the Quarter streetscape as inconspicuously as possible, while leaving the focus on older buildings. The garage is a poor example, with only the most vestigial ornamentation.

The sixty-four room Commercial Hotel was bought in 1886 by Antonio Monteleone, a Sicilian shoemaker who immigrated to New Orleans. He changed the name to the Hotel Monteleone in 1908. The building seen on the left in this circa 1920 view was designed by the architectural firm of Toledano and Wogan, with a terra-cotta facade in the Beaux Arts style. It was the first high-rise hotel in the French Quarter and one of the nation's few family-owned hotels to survive the Great Depression.

Between 1946 and 1964, the left side of the block was gerrymandered
out of the jurisdiction of the Vieux Carré Commission, which ordinarily
would have prevented further tall buildings out of scale with the Old
Quarter. This allowed the construction of the annex on the corner, with the
vertical Monteleone sign in 1954. The hotel has been designated a Literary
Landmark by the Friends of Libraries U.S.A. for having hosted writers such
as Truman Capote, William Faulkner, Eudora Welty, and Tennessee Williams.

Looking down Royal at the intersection with Ursulines Street, circa 1900.
Almost everything is built to pedestrian scale and there are facades strewn
with balconies, galleries, and awnings crowding the narrow streets. The lack
of setback, with houses built flush to the banquette, or sidewalk, and the
profusion of rich cast-iron lace is a visual delight. The rectilinear grid of the
Vieux Carré measures only six by thirteen blocks.

Gone is the quaint granite-block paving and the streetcar tracks, but also
gone is the clutter of overhead electrical wires. The city unfortunately
allowed the company that held the monopoly on public utilities to eliminate
all but the St. Charles Avenue streetcar line by 1964. The modern-day view
shows the downriver end of the Quarter, where tourist-oriented businesses
begin to disappear and the earlier, more residential pattern persists.

The cubic Absinthe House is one of a handful of entresol buildings in New Orleans. A Spanish-colonial innovation brought from Cuba in the late 1700s, entresol buildings usually combined a retail establishment on the ground level, with a residence on the top, and a hidden floor in-between for storage of goods during floods. This middle floor, called the entresol, has a relatively low ceiling and windows made to look like fanlight transoms for the French doors of the first floor.

In the late 1950s, the entresol was removed to create a higher ceiling for the first-floor liquor bar. The anise- or licorice-flavored liqueur absinthe, made with hyssop, veronica, fennel, lemon balm, angelica, and wormwood, was made illegal in the early twentieth century and is no longer sold in the bar bearing its name, though the drink is making a comeback in the Czech Republic, Portugal, Spain, and the United Kingdom.

The so-called Napoleon House, more properly the Girod House, was built in 1814 for Nicholas Girod, the first elected mayor of New Orleans. Although designed after the U.S. purchased Louisiana in 1803, it still has Spanish Creole building features, with a steep hip roof, original flat tiles, and an octagonal belvedere. The more popular name for the building reflects the false tradition that it was intended by the local Creoles as a refuge for the defeated Napoleon Bonaparte.

The building now houses a restaurant replete with classical music and is popular among college students and professors. A winding stairway connects to formerly residential upper floors, now renovated as a reception hall by Joe and Rosie Impastato. Italians, the last major immigrant group to arrive in the 1800s, were forced by poverty to live in the slum that the Old Quarter had become, making Italian Americans today the largest property owners in what is once again the priciest local neighborhood.

019307. HAUNTED HOUSE, NEW ORLEANS, LA.

The Lalaurie House, better known as the Haunted Mansion, is one of the largest and finest homes in the Vieux Carré. It was built in 1831 in a conservative neoclassical style and inherited by Madame Delphine Macarty de Lopez Blanque Lalaurie, the wife of a socially prominent physician. The house was completely redesigned six years later by architect Pierre Edouard Trastour, who added a third floor and converted it to French Empire style.

The current scene looks nearly identical, but a dramatic event in 1834 changed the history of the house forever. All that is known for sure is that a fire broke out in the mansion in 1834, revealing slaves kept chained, tortured, and starved, and some burned to death, in the attic. Ever since, people have speculated wildly about Madame Lalaurie's motives—could it be sex, sadism, or racism?—and insisted that ghosts still haunt the place. Historian Mary Gehman recently revealed a possible motive to the madness—Lalaurie had taken the law into her own hands to interrogate enslaved workers accused of killing her relatives in an uprising on the family plantation.

The view upriver on Dauphine Street, circa 1890, shows the Victorian turret of the now-demolished Mercier Building on Canal Street in the distance. On the left is the 1836 Gardette-LePrêtre House. The wonderful cast-iron galleries, so high above the ground, were added decades later and are supported by dramatic, eighteen-foot columns. The ground level shows false blocking in imitation of stone facing—New Orleans has no native stone.

The cast iron is intact, but the roof of the building on the right has
lost its dormers. A profusion of hanging baskets with lush subtropical
vegetation shows, if the presence of color did not, that this is the
contemporary view. In the distance, the Beaux Arts Ritz-Carlton Hotel,
formerly the Maison Blanche department store (1909), replaces the
Mercier Building.

A sequence of eleven Greek Revival town houses built between 1835 and 1840, the LaBranche Buildings take up most of the little block bounded by Royal Street, St. Peter Street, Exchange Alley, and Pirate's Alley. The cast-iron lace, probably the richest in the Quarter, was an afterthought added decades later. The photograph, made by local commercial photographer Charles Franck, dates from about 1925.

The intricate design of intertwined oak leaves and acorns in the ironwork
retains its charm, but the presence of the colorful hanging baskets again alerts
the viewer that this is the current view. Three quarters of a century on, the
galleries remain the most photographed cast iron in the Quarter. The
picturesque corner has become a magnet for street musicians and jugglers.
The inset shows the Mardi Gras celebrations in 1995, outside the
LaBranche Buildings.

This picture of the back of the cathedral as viewed from Orleans Street was taken circa 1890 by William Henry Jackson (1843–1942). Orleans Street is the axis of the Vieux Carré grid, laid out by French colonial engineer Adrian de Pauger in 1721. It cuts in half the four blocks leading from the cathedral to Congo Square, where, during colonial and antebellum times, the enslaved workers were permitted to sing and dance on Sundays just outside the northern ramparts of the city.

The expanse of Orleans Street, seven feet wider than the Quarter streets, which are twenty-two feet wide, points unmistakably toward the enclosed garden behind the cathedral. This was intended as an oasis of quiet contemplation, overseen by a statue of Christ triumphant and sitting behind an imposing iron fence. Today the same fence serves as just another surface for the display of paintings and drawings for sale by the artists working on Jackson Square.

The Cabildo, the late-colonial city hall, was already more than a century old when this picture was taken in about 1900. Built in the 1790s, in the dying days of Spanish domination, it is the site where France and the United States signed off on the Louisiana Purchase. Note the cast-iron cone in the lower center of the view, which directed horse-drawn transport by demarcating turns in order to prevent the cutting of corners.

In contrast with the relative soberness of a century earlier, the Cabildo now presents a somewhat cluttered, almost gaudy aspect, festooned with eye-catching banners advertising special exhibits of the Louisiana State Museum, for which it serves as the flagship. The State Museum is to the Quarter what the Smithsonian Institution is to the Mall in Washington, D.C., operating many different museum buildings throughout the area.

The first reference to Mardi Gras in Louisiana was in 1699, when Pierre LeMoyne, Sieur d'Iberville, and his crew of explorers observed Shrove Tuesday by naming Mardi Gras Bayou some forty-five miles below the eventual site of New Orleans. The Carnival season originally was celebrated in the colony as it had been in France. However, the influence of Africans and people from the Caribbean meant that the festival gradually evolved into a party infused with drumming, dancing, and wild costumes (see inset). The Anglo-American white elite established after the Purchase formed "krewes," private Carnival clubs that have their own kings and queens and hold masked, themed balls and street parades.

Since its establishment, the Carnival season has been the city's busiest tourist period, when the narrow old streets of the French Quarter are invaded by tens of thousands of revelers. Hundreds of thousands more celebrate on Canal Street and St. Charles Avenue and in the suburbs. Carnival features a huge array of parades, marching bands, balls, and costumers. This image shows the parade of Rex, the King of the Carnival, who first appeared in 1872 and is said to reign for only that one day. The Rex krewe established the official Mardi Gras colors of purple, green, and gold and the official song "If Ever I Cease to Love." For many, the Rex parade is the climax of Mardi Gras.

Bourbon Street is named for the powerful dynasty that ruled in France, Spain, and Naples. Mainly a residential street initially, its commercial side expanded between the 1930s and 1950s, and it garnered a reputation for entertainment and shopping. This photograph shows Bourbon Street looking comparatively respectable in 1946, even though the strip clubs had been moving in since the 1930s.

Bourbon Street is, today, among the most popular tourist attractions in New Orleans and is famed the world over for its commitment to revelry. From five-star hotels to strip joints, the street caters to every taste twenty-four hours a day, three hundred and sixty-five days of the year. In fact, Bourbon Street is one of the biggest and most successful entertainment and retailing areas of the world, with millions of tourists and residents visiting annually.

The French Opera House opened in 1859, just two seasons before the outbreak of the Civil War and at a time when the French-speaking Creole population was in significant decline politically, economically, and culturally. Often garnering artistic success but ever courting bankruptcy, the place ultimately burned down in 1919. No amount of brave talk by the Creoles ever brought its resurrection. This view was taken sometime between 1880 and 1897 by William Henry Jackson.

Today the building in the right foreground remains, but L'Opéra has been replaced by a hotel in a particularly clumsy take on the so-called Vieux Carré Revival style that became popular for new construction in the Quarter in the 1960s. Note the not-quite-Mansard roof. The only influence left from the building's famous predecessor is the slightly indented sidewalk, which originally allowed operagoers to disembark conveniently from their carriages.

Sometimes known as the Le Carpentier House, this imposing mansion on a high pedestal was designed for a wealthy auctioneer in 1826 by the architect François Correjoles. He was the son of refugees from the late eighteenth-century slave rebellion in the French colony of Saint-Domingue, now Haiti. Its Federal stylistic traits, such as the Tuscan columns with exterior stairways extending from either side, reflect growing Anglo-American influences at the time. In fact, the French Quarter has more American-style than Creole-style buildings.

The mansion was rescued from demolition in 1925 and became better known as the Beauregard-Keyes House, after its two most famous residents. Confederate General Pierre Gustave Toutant Beauregard (1818–1893) rented there for fourteen months between 1866 and 1868. In 1944, novelist Frances Parkinson Keyes (1885–1970) leased a portion of the building as her winter residence and New Orleans headquarters. She restored the building and left it to the city in her will.

Just across Chartres Street from the Beauregard-Keyes House is the only surviving French-colonial building in the French Quarter, the Ursuline Convent. It was constructed between 1745 and 1750. Education in New Orleans started with the Roman Catholic Ursuline nuns, who established separate classes for European, African, and Native American girls and women. The convent later became the residence of the archbishop, and the church partly visible on the left was added in 1899.

French-colonial design elements enshrined in the Ursuline Convent parallel those of simple structures in France and Canada in the eighteenth century and include a steep hipped roof, casement windows and doors, and small dormers. The underlying cross-timbering is covered with hard plaster to protect the building from the damp New Orleans climate, but there are no galleries to protect walls from sun or windows from rain. Note the changed portico as compared with the first photo.

The Halle des Boucheries, or Butcher's Market, is the oldest building location in the French Market, though it remains difficult to say which is the oldest structure since they have been rebuilt so many times. The original colonial marketplace was located here, in between the Place d'Armes (now Jackson Square) and the Mississippi River. Since the 1860s, the building has housed the French Market's oldest tenant, Café du Monde.

Still open twenty-four hours a day, seven days a week, Café du Monde is best known for its coffee and beignets. The potent local coffee often incorporates chicory, the roasted root of the endive plant, which gained popularity as a coffee adulterant during the tough times of Civil War and federal occupation. Beignets are rectangles of doughnut dough about three inches square that are deep fried until they puff up and are served doused in confectioner's sugar.

About 1906, when this picture was taken, the Halle des Legumes, or Vegetable Market, of the French Market was engaged in exactly the sort of trade that the name indicates—you can see the tropical fruits for sale in the stall. Many of the vendors were Sicilian, immigrants originally recruited by plantation agents in the 1880s and 1890s as migrant farm workers to compete with the labor of the freedmen (the formerly enslaved people) and their children.

Today the Vegetable Market houses only restaurants and a bar. In front, where the vegetable stands once stood, is a traffic median, or "neutral ground," as it is often called in the South. The gold-leafed statue of Joan of Arc, donated by the French to New Orleans and recently orphaned elsewhere in town by the construction of Harrah's Casino, has been transferred to become a new focus in the market. Only a small part of the gentrified French Market is still used as a farmers' market (see inset).

The first suburb, or faubourg, built downriver from the Quarter was subdivided from the plantation of the white Creole Bernard de Marigny. The town houses shown in this Charles Franck photo of the first block of Frenchmen Street were constructed in the 1850s for Julien Adolphe Lacroix. He was a free Creole of color who once held one-sixth of all real estate owned by free black New Orleanians, the wealthiest free black population in the nation before the Civil War.

Frenchman Street still forms an obtuse angle off Decatur Street, helping to conform the layout of the Marigny suburb to the Vieux Carré grid. The ground floors of the Lacroix Buildings still house retail stores, and the second-floor and attic levels still serve as residences. However, the neighborhood now largely serves a gay population. Trendy dining and other "alternative" businesses have replaced Julien Lacroix's original grocery store.

As late as two years after World War II, when this Franck photograph was taken, New Orleans was still crisscrossed with tracks for nonpolluting electrical trolleys. The scourge of yellow fever, malaria, and other terrible epidemics throughout the nineteenth century gave rise to the Mortuary Chapel, on the left, designed by Gurlie and Guillot. A chapel of the dead, the only living persons it sheltered were the members of the clergy who were attending the deceased.

Partly at the urging of the auto industry, midcentury civic boosters picked
buses to replace streetcars. To add an extra lane to street traffic in both
directions, the neutral ground was narrowed, the trees removed, and the
lampposts relocated. In the twentieth century, the Mortuary Chapel
successively has served Irish, Sicilian, Filipino, and Hispanic immigrants,
and is now called Our Lady of Guadalupe. Just beyond are Congo Square and
Armstrong Park.

This classic view, circa 1900, shows a typical alley of aboveground tombs in the oldest surviving cemetery in town, St. Louis Number One. In the background is one of the largest and most elaborate society tombs, the Italia Tomb. The old Creole burial ground received an influx of immigrant Italian deceased in the late nineteenth and early twentieth centuries. Storyville, the notorious turn-of-the-century red-light district, surrounds the cemetery.

A century later, almost nothing but the immediate surroundings seems to have changed. No longer in a red-light district, the cemetery is but steps away from a large public housing development built in the 1940s. The aboveground burial is necessitated by poor soil conditions, low elevation, a high water table, and flooding.

The Ursuline nuns donated this land near the Claude Tremé plantation main house for St. Augustine Roman Catholic Church. It served the Creole population, white, free black, and enslaved, of Faubourg Tremé which, along with Marigny, is one of the two earliest Creole suburbs. The church was home to the association of lay people in support of the Sisters of the Holy Family, one of only three historically black orders of Catholic nuns in the U.S.

You have to look past the continued clutter of overhead wires and the stark, all-white paint job to appreciate the enduring beauty of French architect J. N. B. de Pouilly's 1842 design, for the same environmental conditions that promote aboveground burial also inhibit the burial of electrical lines. The cupola is campanile-shaped, like the cupolas that originally graced the towers of the same architect's St. Louis Cathedral (replaced by the neo-Gothic steeples we know today).

Charles Franck took this bird's-eye view at the end of the Great Depression from the roof of the then-new Municipal Auditorium. The auditorium fronts Place Congo, out of view below the lower foreground, where African music and dance were preserved. Along with the mastery in New Orleans of European music and musical instruments, this enabled the city to combine two traditions to form what eventually became the quintessentially American music, jazz.

Back atop the auditorium today, the expanse of Orleans Street still effortlessly leads the eye toward the cathedral. The overall aspect of the scene has changed little, except for things such as the orange scaffolding on the cathedral. Rarely has an early- to mid-nineteenth-century town survived to the degree that it has here. Of the nation's three oldest historic districts, only those of Charleston and New Orleans are actual restorations. Colonial Williamsburg, Virginia, is a reconstruction.

The idea to build the chapel was conceived during the yellow fever epidemic of 1868, when a German priest, Father Peter Leonard Thevis, prayed for the intercession of St. Roch. A French nobleman (1295–1327), St. Roch worked among plague sufferers in Italy during the Middle Ages. Made of brick in the Gothic Revival style, the chapel was completed in 1876, the year of the withdrawal of the occupying federal troops from the South.

The St. Roch Cemetery was modeled after the Campo Santo dei Tedeschi, or Holy Field of the Germans, near St. Peter's in Rome. The subtle relief of the building's German-style brickwork, so evident in the circa 1905 view, today appears obscured by an impasto of white stucco. The chapel became noted for the ex-votos on display inside, including castoff crutches and plaster casts of human limbs, attesting to cures through St. Roch's intervention.

The building was constructed on the outer edge of the Faubourg Macarty area, downriver of the original city in 1826 for plantation owner Joseph Lombard, Jr. With its double-pitched hip roof, narrow tapered columns, small dormers, shuttered French doors, and deep gallery across the front, it resembles a French-Caribbean plantation main house. However, like other manor houses that appeared locally from the mid-1820s, it is smaller in scale and has lower basement elevations than such West Indian predecessors.

The Lombard House is now the last remaining example in New Orleans of
a Creole manor house. Not all of the good-looking recent refurbishments
appear to be completely authentic. The shallow storage space below the
house has been enclosed and shuttered windows have been added to the
spaces between the piers. The original front center dormer now also sports
shutters, and the house has a new, flattering tropical color scheme.

The foot of Canal served as a major terminus for intermodal transportation, with passenger trains, streetcar lines, and waterborne traffic all converging here. On this day in 1900, a crowd is shown waiting to greet the arrival of the boat of Rex, the King of Carnival. The day was Lundi Gras, the Monday preceding Mardi Gras, or Fat Tuesday, Rex's one day of rule. The custom ran from the mid-1870s to 1917 and was revived in 1987.

The scene at the foot of Canal is just as busy, but it is not the same kind of busy. The Canal Street Ferry still travels between here and Algiers—you can see the landing at left—and people still throng the area, but mainly for the shopping, entertainment, and tourism. Note on the right the blue glass wedge of the Aquarium of the Americas and on the left the twin cupolas on the roof of Harrah's Casino.

United Liquor was one of many shipping and importing firms that once occupied irregularly shaped blocks immediately upriver from the foot of Canal. In 1968, it, among other buildings, was replaced by the Rivergate Convention Center. An engineering marvel of the time, the Rivergate had a remarkably sculptural roof structure that required relatively few slender support columns so as not to obstruct the space for setting up the conventions.

The development of the mammoth Ernest N. Morial Convention Center, starting with a first phase built for the 1984 Louisiana World Exposition, made the much smaller Rivergate obsolete. It was demolished to make way for Harrah's Casino, which opened in 1999. An almost arbitrary blend of vaguely neoclassical design elements, Harrah's has the advantage of dramatic bas-reliefs in the pediments. The ones on the Canal Street pediment are from designs by the renowned local painter George Dureau.

The Custom House became a government boondoggle and the work undertaken in 1849 did not reach completion until 1881. Basically a Greek Revival design, the exception to that pattern is the quartet of giant granite Egyptian Revival columns repeated on each of the four facades. The columns are surmounted by papyrus capitals that support an entablature with a massive cast-iron cornice covered with lotuses and other motifs associated with Ancient Egyptian, rather than Greek or Roman architecture.

What was one of the biggest buildings of its day is now dwarfed by the
Marriott Hotel to the left. The Custom House today is a federal building
with limited access. The Audubon Institute, which runs the nearby
Aquarium of the Americas, is planning to open an insectarium here.

Built in 1821, this is the oldest surviving structure on Canal Street. It initially resembled the Napoleon House four blocks downriver on Chartres Street in the Quarter. It was remodeled in 1899, but the original window placement, as shown in this 1920 view by Charles Franck, remained unchanged. The remodeling mainly involved the addition of pressed metal lintels and a heavy parapet that partially obscures the hip roof and dormers.

This looks to be just about the most antique Wendy's anywhere. The fast food restaurant replaces the barber shop, hat shop, cigar shop, and shoe repair shop that were there in 1920. The overhang that sheltered the corner is gone, but a smaller covered entrance has been inserted in the middle of the Canal Street facade. It is dwarfed by the Marriott next door.

Canal Street became the dividing line between the Creole Quarter on the right and the American business district on the left. For much of its history, one of Canal Street's most prominent landmarks was the Henry Clay Statue at the intersection, with Royal Street on the right and St. Charles on the left. William Henry Jackson's photograph, taken in about 1890, is full of period detail. Note the advertisement for the French Opera.

A streetcar on the St. Charles Avenue line runs one block along Canal before turning back upriver. The olive-colored cars were the last to run until recently, when the city won federal money to return streetcars to the length of Canal. The new red car line runs on the Canal Street neutral ground—the planned canal that gave the street its name was never built—and along the river from the Convention Center to the downriver end of the Quarter.

The deluxe autos still present in the financial district in this early-1930s Franck photo of Carondelet off Canal Street show pre-Depression prosperity. On the left, dominating the view then as now, is the twenty-three-story American Bank Building. Designed by architect Moise Goldstein, its elegant Art Deco setbacks are faced in granite and limestone. Dead in the distant middle is the circular temple atop the Hibernia National Bank, also twenty-three stories and designed in the Italian Renaissance manner.

Missing from the right in the new view is the now-defunct firm of Junius Hart, one of the major publishers of local sheet music in the nineteenth century. Music publishing died out here as the business moved to Chicago and New York. Note the 1930s-style modernization of the Corinthian columns of the building in the left foreground (originally the City Bank and Trust Company, 1905).

The Chess, Checkers, and Whist Club, with its high-Victorian corner cupola and eyebrow-like hood molds over arched windows is shown in this Detroit Publishing Company photo (circa 1903). Like other gentlemen's clubs along the upriver side of Canal Street, it traditionally erected viewing stands for its members' and their families' enjoyment of parades during carnival season. Looking down Baronne Street to the left is the first Grunewald Hotel, a six-story building dating from 1893.

In 1908, the Grunewald built a high-rise annex on University Place. The original, six-story hotel on Baronne was replaced in the mid-1930s by another big annex. It is this second annex that towers over what replaced the Chess, Checkers, and Whist Club, the 1938 Walgreen's. Recently gutted, rebuilt, and expanded to the right behind new twin brick facades that blend well with the original, neon-rich facade, Walgreen's is one of the few and finest Art Deco designs in town.

This circa 1890 image depicts the Greek Revival–style Mechanics Institute (1856), which rose to international infamy after the Civil War in the bloody Mechanics Institute Riot of 1866. White and black men were meeting there to draw up a new state constitution to grant black men the right to vote, when the police yielded to a pro-Confederate mob that broke in and killed many delegates. The riot helped precipitate the more punitive, radical phase of Reconstruction. This print was originally published as a stereograph.

In the Institute's stead is the Fairmont Hotel, formerly called the Roosevelt Hotel, which originally was the first, 1908 annex to the Grunewald Hotel. Known as the Fairmont since 1965, some four decades later it is still called the Roosevelt by most locals. In its heyday, the Roosevelt was New Orleans headquarters for the Kingfish, Louisiana's magnetic and notorious governor Huey Long. Today the Fairmont is the only unionized hotel in New Orleans.

About 1913, the roof of the Grunewald Hotel (the hotel's 1908 annex
fronting on University Place) became the outlook for a series of photographs
that the Detroit Publishing Company made to form a wonderful panorama
of downtown New Orleans. This panel in the series shows the Beaux-Arts
terra-cotta facade of the Maison Blanche Department Store (1909) on the
left. In the lower right is the cupola of the Chess, Checkers, and Whist Club.
The Quarter is in the right background.

Adaptive use is becoming an ever larger part of preserving the historically important old buildings on Canal Street. In 2002, Maison Blanche became the exclusive Ritz-Carlton Hotel. Space on the ground floor was redeveloped as a high-end retail galleria, with the other twelve stories given over to hotel rooms. All along this stretch of Canal Street, businesses are being diverted from local trade to tourist-oriented ventures.

The next panel in the 1913 panorama points toward the foot of Canal and again mostly shows the French Quarter side of the street. Above the diagonal path of the street, a number of Vieux Carré landmarks are easy to spot, such as the pearly-white terra-cotta of the high-rise Hotel Monteleone. The D. H. Holmes Department Store, also white-colored, stands out in the lower left. Notice the lettering that runs down the middle of the six-bay facade.

D. H. Holmes has been adapted, like its biggest retail competitor Maison Blanche, as a hotel called the Chateau Sonesta. It may be difficult to spot, though it stands out just as white as it did ninety years ago. However, the six single-window bays on the facade have been replaced with three three-window bays. One block down, the Astor Hotel, a largely new building made to appear a century older, blocks all but the penthouse and roof of the Monteleone.

The next panel in the 1913 panorama shows just a bit of Canal Street in the upper left, where you can spot the U.S. Custom House and, just above it, along the Vieux Carré batture, smokestacks of now-gone sugar refineries. In the lower right is the dome of Jesuit Church. The rest shows the American business district then still rapidly developing, with the high-rise Whitney National Bank under construction.

Cast in deep shadow just right of the bottom center, the dome of Jesuit Church looks about the same. This is remarkable when you learn that the entire building was demolished because of structural problems in 1928 to be rebuilt two years later. Almost everything else is different. At the center, Place St. Charles juts up among several skyscrapers that transformed the skyline of the Central Business District toward the end of the previous century.

This view up Baronne was taken by Charles Frank circa 1926. On the left is the original antebellum Moresque-style Jesuit Church and, beyond it, the Jesuit-owned Pére Marquette Building (1925), a subtly neo-Gothic skyscraper. At the center is New Orleans Public Service, Inc. (NOPSI), the local public utilities company, which was housed in this Mansard-style building dating from the 1870s. On the right are clothing stores and the Crescent Theater, which presented both movies and vaudeville.

The rebuilt Jesuit Church reuses much of the original antebellum material, including ornate cast-iron pews inside. A recent renovation of the Pére Marquette Building resulted in the gutting of its intact 1920s shopping gallery. In place of NOPSI's Reconstruction-era French Renaissance Revival building is the Art Deco-style Sears Roebuck and Co., now a Travelodge. The sadly blank 1960s facade on the right is a poor substitute for the varied turn-of-the-century buildings it replaced.

Misty air glistens from electric lights coming on at dusk on Canal Street (circa 1930). Maison Blanche (MB) is surmounted by tall broadcasting towers for its own WSMB radio station. Two massive silent-era movie houses, the Saenger (1927) and Loew's (1926), span the whole width of the block on Canal between Rampart and Basin Streets. Nearby were several other theaters, of which at least one, the Orpheum (1918), still survives. The Louisiana Philharmonic Orchestra now performs there.

The contemporary view, shot on a much clearer evening, shows the Canal Street neutral ground torn up for the reinstallation of streetcar tracks. Toward the foot of Canal, new buildings crowd the sky. Significantly, most of them are hotels, at least above the first story or so. In the case of Canal Place, mostly hidden in this view by the Marriott, the first three floors are a shopping mall.

The Saenger is shown nearing completion in 1927. It was one of the largest and most lavish picture palaces built in the South toward the end of the silent-movie era. Architect Emile Weil designed the interior in sumptuous Renaissance style to make audiences feel as though they were watching the movie in a courtyard set amid ornate antique Italian palazzi. The ceiling was painted to look like the night sky, with twinkling stars and moveable clouds.

Until the 1960s, unlike other large downtown movie houses, the Saenger did not permit African-American people even in the balcony. After racial desegregation, the balcony was divided off as the separate, reserved-seats-only Saenger Orleans, where that last blast of big movie musicals and other road show movies were presented. Since then, the balcony and ground levels have been reunited. Today the Saenger rarely shows movies, serving instead as a venue for live performances.

You hear a lot but you do not see a lot about Storyville, the renowned red-light district. You can see the ribald portraits of prostitutes and yet get little sense of what the district looked like overall. This bird's-eye view is extracted from a single, 360-degree panoramic photograph by local photographer George Prince in 1919. Storyville runs diagonally along Basin Street in the upper left.

When the panorama was made, Storyville was already dead, shut down at the request of the United States Navy during World War I. Servicemen were being mugged, rolled, and, sometimes, killed—it had to come to an end. Occupying the Basin Street strip today are the back buildings of Krauss Department Store, now empty, and public housing. On the lower right, is the Audubon Building (1910), another of the solid row of Beaux Arts facades of glazed terra cotta that make the 900 downriver block of Canal so attractive.

Picturesque, yes, but the smells from the turning basin of the New Basin Canal were often potent. Between 1832 and 1838, this often stagnant ditch that cut through disease-infested swampland cost thousands of Irish and German immigrant lives in the digging. The Americans wanted to connect their part of town by water to Lake Pontchartrain to compete with the Creoles' Old Basin Canal at the back of the Quarter.

The New Basin Canal was filled in and replaced by the Pontchartrain Expressway in the 1950s. Rather than directly imitate the historical image, this image was taken from way above the original viewpoint to clearly show the location's current use, for auto traffic and parking for the civic center along Loyola Avenue. This is a government district to which city hall and other city and state offices were moved in the 1960s.

The view in 1900 is tumultuous. It shows the crowds at city hall for the arrival of the parade float of Rex, the King of Carnival, on Mardi Gras day. Now called Gallier Hall, for architect James Gallier, Sr., the antebellum building (1845–1850) is the finest example of Greek Revival style to survive in a city that, in its heyday, had more Grecian temples than ancient Athens.

Today's sleepy, golden-lit view discloses that the political action moved to the current city hall, a 1960s green glass box some seven blocks farther from the river. Only later in the day might the Gallier Hall doors open to one of a myriad of gatherings—civic, artistic, or educational—seeking its sophisticated atmosphere. Notice how the brilliant design crams all the requisite classical elements into a typically tiny and narrow New Orleans lot.

The Central Business District had the greatest number of Victorian-style buildings in the city. The style was often worked in porous stone and other materials more appropriate to northern climes than damp New Orleans. The neo-Gothic, fortresslike Masonic Temple (1891) was built from a twenty-year-old design by architect James Freret. It stood until 1926, when the then-flush Freemasons opted for bigger headquarters.

Jutting dramatically amid newer skyscrapers, this is actually the third Masonic structure to occupy the site, the first being Galliers's Commercial Exchange (1845). The present-day, eighteen-story Masonic Building was designed by architect Sam Stone in Gothic Modern style. Little survives of the spectacular historical theme rooms, Egyptian, Greek, Roman, Medieval, and the like, that graced many floors, though a theater survives as a lecture hall.

As late as 1926 on Poydras and Baronne Streets, there is still a horse cart, as well as a cyclist and two models of streetcars. The view by Charles Franck shows the American Rennaisance–style Hotel De Soto's original orientation to have been on Baronne. The architectural firm of Toledano and Wogan designed the nine-story steel structure as the Denechaud Hotel in 1906. The first two, rusticated floors are faced in terra cotta.

The ornate cornice that crowned the De Soto appears reduced to a steel skeleton in the old view and is entirely missing in the new view of the hotel, now named Le Pavillon. In the mid-1960s, Poydras was widened by demolition on the downriver side. The six-bay, two-story facade seen abutting the De Soto in the lower right of the old view was eliminated. In its place is the two-bay-deep motor entrance with a Texas-size emblem that reorients the hotel to Poydras.

Charles Franck's own shop appears on the downriver side, 900 block, Poydras Street. It was of one of seven three-story stores built in a row in 1845. They were made of brick made on the north shore of Lake Pontchartrain, which has the right ingredients. The locally made brick is orange and crumbly and requires protection from the elements in the form of stucco. These stores originally were merely painted and stenciled.

From the same viewpoint today, you see only the base of the thirty-seven-story neo-Deco Louisiana Land and Exploration Tower, a late result of the oil boom that ended in the early 1980s. Almost everything on this side of Poydras is new because of the widening. The sculptures in front, David and The Lute Player (1988), are by Mexican artist Enrique Aférez, whose career has spanned eight decades from the 1920s to the twenty-first century.

Architect Emile Weil's redbrick Crane Company warehouse was nearing completion when Franck took this picture in 1921. The Fulton Bag and Cotton Mill, also made of brick, was designed by architect Sam Stone in 1909. It later served as the Krauss Department Store warehouse. A century ago, this section of town reached its zenith as a manufacturing center, producing, among other things, cigars, metal bedsteads, heavy fabric for awnings and sails, and rope and twine.

Even shorn of its original pyramidal roof, the fine brick tower of the Krauss warehouse remains a landmark for motorists arriving from the West Bank of the Mississippi across the Crescent City Connection. The area is commonly called the Warehouse District, not taking into account its history in manufacturing, and is mainly residential, with trendy apartments and pricey condominiums proving the efficacy of adaptive use for historic preservation.

This image, originally published as a stereopair, was taken by Thomas Lilienthal in about 1867 from the roof of St. Patrick's Church on Camp Street, which was built between 1838 and 1840 for Irish immigrants. Until then, the city was small enough to have only one Catholic Church parish, the cathedral. Julia Street runs diagonally from the lower left, and along it, you can see Julia Street Row (1832–1833), sometimes called the Thirteen Sisters.

A neighborhood-within-a-neighborhood in the Warehouse District is the Arts District. Access to the roof of St. Patrick's having grown ever more precarious, Julia Street and its environs, now the main art gallery street, must be seen here from a few doors down and the other side of Camp Street. The American Federal style of the identical redbrick town houses of Julia Street Row would not be out of place in Baltimore or Philadelphia.

More row buildings, this time six commercial structures with stone block fronts on Carondelet, the street named for the last Spanish colonial governor. Originally numbering eight, they are among the few mid-nineteenth-century granite stores left here. Built to a design by architect George Purves, the row received its only local accent in the cast-iron gallery added to the corner building a few years after construction.

Renovation gently jostles restoration in the first three stores upriver. The
gallery has been stripped from the corner store. Both square and arched
windows have been restored to the original number of lights, with French
casements and Gothic style lintels. However, the granite has been painted a
terra-cotta color, and the cornice has been extended upward in order to
define these three as forming one business.

The plastered-brick, Greek Revival church was built in 1851 as a replacement for the burned-out Edward McGehee Charge, the first Methodist Episcopal church in New Orleans. The Ionic portico and deep entablature of the original design have survived, but the original center Greek-form cupola collapsed not very long after construction. The original hip roof is hidden behind the temple-like facade. The "Glad U Kum" sign may be welcoming Masonic conventioneers in April 1910.

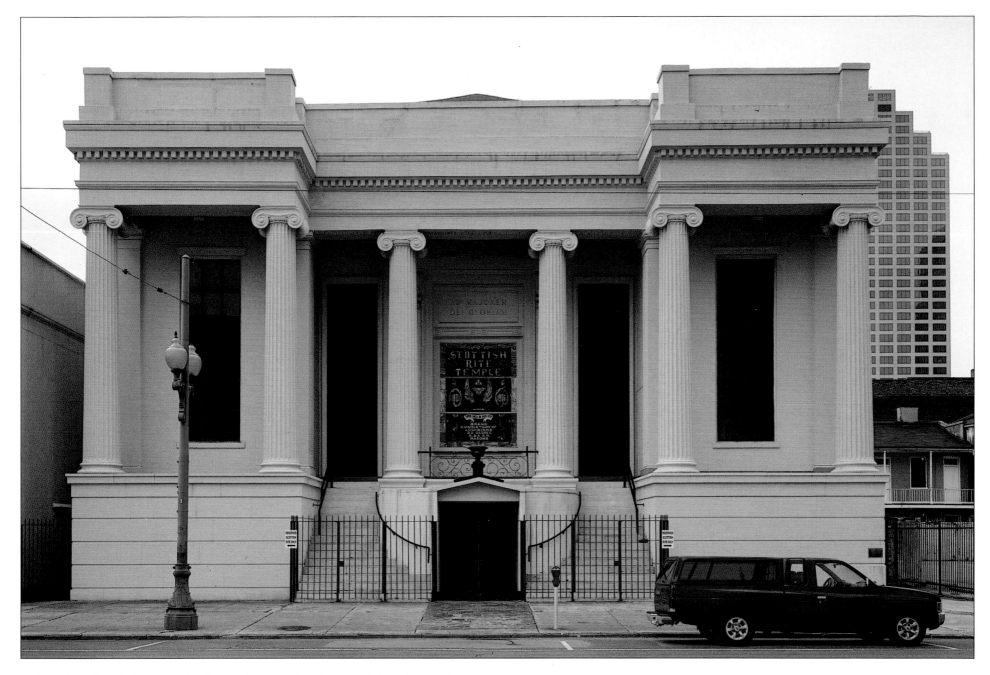

When the church became the Scottish Rite Temple in 1906, architect Sam Stone designed a number of changes to the facade. The Freemasons requested a stained-glass window in place of the original front door. New entrances were added on either side, with an additional, particularly clumsy one, inserted into the base. Since then, further changes have been made to the base, the staircases, and the transom above the stained-glass window.

Among the earliest photographs herein, this circa 1858 view by J. Dearborn Edwards shows the American Fire Company of 1837 on the right. At the center is a pole for spotting the locations of fires and the double facade of architect William Freret's antebellum Washington Artillery Hall. Five years after the picture was taken, Union troops occupied both buildings. The hall burned down shortly after. Its facade ultimately was relocated across from Jackson Square, where it survived until 1972.

Just about all you can see from the original viewpoint in this new view is the firehouse. The rest is obscured by trees. The building continued in use as a firehouse until 1960, when it became an electronics business. It remains unclear when the arched entrance was added. Many of the other buildings in the historical view have survived to become offices, and the street still maintains its antebellum scale and character.

As a country manor and one of the earliest homes built in the American sector, the 1815 Delord-Sarpy House was oriented to the river, not the street. In this circa 1920 Franck photo, it has lost all of its grounds and is jostled on both sides by newer buildings. This shows the side of the house, with the front galleries, eight columns in width, to the left, supported by box pillars of brick below with round columns of wood above.

The Delord-Sarpy House survived to become the oldest building upriver from
canal until the building of the highway in the 1950s. The house overlapped
the planned location of this off-ramp for what is now called the Crescent
City Connection. Despite entreaties to spare the house, neither politicians
nor the public were ready for the concept of economic development through
historic preservation. Instead, they chose the lowest-cost solution to move
cars in from the West Bank.

The red-sandstone, Romanesque Revival–style Howard Memorial Library, shown here in about 1900, was built in 1888. The design is by Louisiana-born architect Henry Hobson Richardson, who studied in New Orleans but never built anything here, instead achieving fame in the North. His unused plan for a library in Saginaw, Michigan, was developed two years after his death and used to design a research library in New Orleans, specializing in Louisiana history.

Richardsonian Romanesque is the only architectural style to come, at least
in part, from the Crescent City to influence architecture elsewhere—not
counting the imitation French Quarters in Disney parks. Today the Howard
Memorial Library is incorporated into the Ogden Museum of Southern Art
and is part of a museum district forming toward the lake end of the Arts
District, along with the Contemporary Arts Center (blocked in this view
behind the library building) and the D-Day Museum just visible on the right.

An important landmark adjacent to the Ogden Museum is Lee Circle. A number of fine, older buildings, now gone, once surrounded the circle. Even a facility as mundane as a gas station had to be given high style to fit in. A rich Spanish Colonial Revival design, this Texaco gas station and garage was built in 1926 to conform to the curve and prestige of the circle.

Gone is the palace. Today's suburban-looking Texaco station is almost indistinguishable from any other. Looming to the left is the 1966 Plaza Tower, at the time of construction the world's tallest marble-faced building. Other important buildings no longer on or near the Circle were the combination Byzantine-Romanesque Temple Sinai (Charles Lewis Hillger, 1872) and the copper-domed Beaux Arts main branch of the Public Library (Diboll, Owen, and Goldstein, 1908).

The first or second statue in the U.S.—there is some debate on the subject—
to honor an actual woman, rather than merely serving as an allegorical figure,
is the Margaret Statue. Sculpted by Alexander Doyle, the 1884 statue depicts
Margaret Haughery, an Irish immigrant orphaned within four years of her
arrival in America, who lost her husband and newborn child to yellow fever
in New Orleans, and yet survived to become a great benefactor to widows
and orphans.

The Margaret Statue still dominates Margaret Place today. Haughery's features of white Carrara marble are dulled by humidity and rain but the stone appears to gleam against the lush, dark greenery that has sprung up around it. The large fence widely surrounding it in this century-old view has been replaced by one of much smaller circumference. The 1840 Female Orphan Asylum still stands behind it but is now obscured.

Samuel Hastings bought most of the lake side of the 1800 block of Magazine Street in 1853 and 1854. In 1860, he had architect Thomas Gillam design and build this row of thirteen two-story Greek Revival buildings. Following nineteenth-century New Orleans custom, they combined businesses on the ground level with residences on the second. The Franck photo also shows the later addition of sumptuous cast-iron galleries.

Gone are all but one section of the galleries and eight of the original twenty-two front dormers after a fire gutted almost the entire block shortly before this color shot was taken. The view dramatizes the need to protect buildings in a place such as New Orleans that has high concentrations of old wood in construction. What fire and hurricanes have not destroyed often has been undermined by ravenous Formosan termites that were inadvertently imported during the Korean War.

The somewhat subdued neo-Romanesque style of this 1896 building on the river side of St. Charles at Jackson Avenue is not really Richardsonian. The base is heavily rusticated, but the other surfaces are both plainer and more rectilinear than the typically extreme and varied style. The place served as the Harmony Club, a Jewish organization, then the Young Men's Hebrew Association, and finally, when this picture was taken in 1925, the headquarters of Standard Oil of Louisiana.

The previous structure was razed in the 1950s to be replaced by this twelve-story apartment building. The demand for apartments along "the Avenue" has prompted the wholesale demolition of old buildings up and down the street until city planners finally put on the breaks during the late twentieth century. Note on the right the Art Deco office building that appeared around the block on Jackson Avenue at the start of the 1930s.

J. Dearborn Edwards' 1858 image depicts the Greek Revival–style Buckner House in the Lower Garden District when it was all of about two years old. It was designed by Lewis E. Reynolds—architect of the famed Stanton Hall antebellum home in Natchez, Mississippi—for wealthy cotton broker Henry Sullivan Buckner. Note the tracks in Jackson Avenue for the horse-drawn streetcars of the day. The neighborhood originally was the independent American town of Lafayette. Lafayette on the Mississippi above New Orleans is not to be confused with the city of Lafayette in Acadiana to the west.

Today's Garden District was annexed by the city of New Orleans after the
Americans ended the division of the Crescent City into three separate
municipalities (1836–1852). Today's scene is so overgrown with giant live
oaks and other greenery that little more than the Doric columns and the
broad cast-iron and wooden galleries can be seen.

Depicted is the Adams House owned by Boston-born insurance executive Thomas A. Adams. How countrified the Garden District looks here in this circa 1858 Edwards photograph. The streets are mud, fences and signs are made of wood, and everything is surrounded by lots of space. What a contrast this makes with the typical aspect of a cramped Creole-style neighborhood, where buildings are built flush to the banquette.

Here is the intersection of Prytania and Fourth Streets today. Gone is the
Adams House, but the current home still sits on a garden-filled lot that
is delightfully large by New Orleans standards. The biggest changes come in
the form of overhead electrical lines, cast-iron fences, asphalt-paved streets,
and concrete sidewalks. The greatest challenge the Garden District faces
today is not in this view—the proximity of pronounced poverty amid all
this wealth.

Audubon Place is on the lake side of St. Charles, the grand American residential avenue of New Orleans. One of very few private streets in the city, it was only about a decade old when this Detroit Publishing Company view appeared in around 1906. The broad and imposing rusticated Richardsonian Romanesque gateway is by architect Thomas Sully. Next door is Tulane University, which was established after Reconstruction as an all-white, all-male institution.

Now Tulane University serves all, but Audubon Place remains an exclusive gated community. The original gatehouses are disused, and greater security is achieved through the insertion of a new guard post and traffic bars in between. The tile roofs have held up well, and the palm tree on the left and the oak on the right have grown to dramatic heights. You always notice how green New Orleans is when arriving back by air.

Five Ford, Bacon, and Davis streetcars are lined up for dispatch in this 1899 view of the Carrollton Streetcar Barn. The barn was in the American city of Carrollton (as it was previously known), annexed by New Orleans in 1874. The facility was built by the Berlin Iron Bridge Company in 1893, when the transit company began to switch from horse-drawn to electrical streetcars. The process was nearly complete by the time of the photograph.

The neighborhood is now called Riverbend, for the turn the Mississippi takes at St. Charles and Carrollton Avenues. The governmental Regional Transit Authority took over from NOPSI and discarded many streetcars. The agency is now hard pressed to assemble enough cars and car parts from as far away as Australia to make the new red line along Canal Street to City Park. Today's car barn is as much a refabrication facility as a transportation center.

Gayarré Place is a little triangular park formed by the intersection of
Esplanade Avenue, the grand Creole residential avenue of New Orleans,
and Bayou Road, the original land route to Bayou St. John and on to Lake
Pontchatrain. The statue of Ceres on its terra-cotta pedestal is one of the
few things to have survived from the 1884–1885 World's Industrial and
Cotton Centennial Exposition, which led to the development of Audubon
Park and Zoo.

The World's Fair was held uptown, but Gayarré Place is on the way to the downtown City Park, the largest in tightly laid out New Orleans, where land is at such a premium. Time has severely affected the sculpture. The base is sprouting vegetation. Ceres, missing most of an arm in the circa 1910 view, is now missing the smaller figures that once sat at her feet.

One of the gems of City Park, the fifth-largest urban park in the nation, is the 1907 concrete peristyle which is sometimes called the Lion Pavilion for the sculptures by Pietro Ghiloni that flank its broad stairs. Architect Paul Andry conceived the building as an elegant platform for dancing alongside the last remnant of Bayou Metairie. An Ionic colonnade sits below a raised parapet of pinwheels between piers that gave added height to the entablature without appearing to be too heavy.

Calm waters still calmly reflect the poised neoclassicism of City Park.
The peristyle required major repairs in 1919, 1937, 1947, and 1989, because
of leakage on the roof and the elaborate cutwork parapet eventually had to
go. Close examination reveals faint swag-shaped stains along the new, blank
parapet of the building made by the electrically lighted garland draped there
during the annual celebration in the Oaks Christmas display.

Metairie Cemetery was built during Reconstruction in 1872–1873, along the former route of the Metairie Race Course. Some of the best land around the city, including this natural high ground formed by Bayou Metairie, has been given over for cities of the dead. In a city full of aboveground tombs, this is the cemetery that has the most spectacular collection of them. This scene was captured about a century ago.

Metairie Cemetery is replete with examples of virtually every mid- to late-nineteenth-century architectural style imaginable, including Greek Revival, Gothic Revival, Italianate, Moresque, and, even, neo-Egyptian styles. Among the famous people buried here are P. B. S. Pinchback, the first black governor in the U.S., and jazzman Louis Prima of "Jump, Jive, and Wail" fame.

The tour of the Crescent City ends as it started, along water. Having commenced at the "beautiful crescent" site on the river of the original colonial village, the tour concludes at its northernmost point, the Southern Yacht Club on Lake Pontchartrain. Tracing its roots to the Gold Challenge Cup race held in Pass Christian, Mississippi, in 1849, it is the second oldest yacht club in the U.S. The Lake Pontchartrain clubhouse depicted was built in 1899.

The view a century later is relatively cluttered. The 1899 clubhouse was renovated in 1920. By 1949, however, it was so deteriorated that it had to be replaced by the present structure, which itself saw some modernization in the 1960s. The original location was on the left bank of the New Basin Canal. The current site appears to be farther to the west in West End and contrasts sharply in style and materials with the almost all-wooden building of 1899.

# INDEX